Soul
REVOLUTION

Makhado R. Ramabulana

Inquiries and Book Orders should be addressed to:

Great Writers Media
Email: info@greatwritersmedia.com
Phone: 877-600-5469

ISBN: 978-1-959493-86-0 (sc)
ISBN: 978-1-959493-87-7 (ebk)

Acknowledgements

This book is a culmination of a cultural and spiritual evolution in my life, shaped, molded and coerced by some of the most interesting, talented and gifted souls ever found at one place.

Born at Sandile Dikeni's House of Truth at Papas, came of age at the late Richard Ishmael's Off the Wall sessions at Off-Moroka Café Africana. For those brave souls who shared in its upbringing in particular the late Richard, Jeff and Sandile (may their souls rest in peace), Primrose, Peter, Jade and everybody who was a participant at the Off-Moroka open mike sessions; this is your book. The years were 2001 until 2004, a good season.

And not forgetting those who believed and encouraged that those hastily scribbled thoughts and ideas are worthy their day in the light my lovely wife Julia and not forgetting my friends Dawn, Themba and my editor Pascal Siphugu; thanks for your dedication and believes in the art of the possible.

Contents

Cinna The Poet

CINNA THE POET
What is my name? Whither am I going? Where do I dwell? Am I married or a bachelor? Then, to answer every man directly and briefly, wisely and truly: wisely I say, I am a bachelor.

Second Citizen
That's as much to say, they are fools that marry: You'll bear me a bang for that, I fear proceed; directly.

CINNA THE POET
Directly, I am going to Caesar's funeral.

First Citizen
As a friend or an enemy?

CINNA THE POET
As a friend.

Second Citizen
That matter is answered Directly.

Fourth Citizen
For your dwelling, —briefly.

CINNA THE POET
Briefly, I dwell by the Capitol.

Third Citizen
Your name, sir, truly.

CINNA THE POET
Truly, my name is Cinna.

First Citizen
Tear him to pieces, he is a conspirator.

CINNA THE POET
I am Cinna the poet, I am Cinna the poet.

Fourth Citizen
Tear him for his bad verses, tear him for his bad verses…"

ACT 3. Scene III - JULIUS CEASER
WILLIAM SHAKESPEARE

One Of Us

I am one of us
You offered me a chance to become one of you
You offered to invite, show and teach
me how to become one of you
I am one of us

You promised to teach me how to dress,
walk, behave, think and be one of you
You promised to school me, educate me, civilize me,
To become one of you
I am one of us

You put before me the beauty, the worldly knowledge,
And the glory of it all
You gave me a chance to become a citizen of
the world, to be one with the rest of them
I am one of us

You told me how unfriendly, how unpleasant and how
Dangerous this world can be
But! I am just one of us

Ridicule

It is my greatest phobia, my infancy was structured on it
My childhood was built around it,
My adulthood was cemented on it
I was taught from the very first day, to be like others
Never to say how I felt, never to do as I felt,
Never to behave as I felt, to always do as others do

Children teased me when I couldn't play as they did,
Classmates laughed at me for thinking the way I did,
Colleagues discouraged me from raising my
objections, I learned to keep quite, shut up, stay
mum and tow the line, to always do as others do

I learned to suppress my thoughts, to forgo my ideas,
to be oblivious to my feelings, disregard my instincts,
To kill my dreams and never to follow my heart,
I learned to be heartless, loveless, emotionless and proud
I lost my resolve, my courage, my humility, and my ideal.
I was born without fear of who I am,
I learned to always do as others do

A Bubble Of Emotions

When I can't feel, can't touch, can't hear, can't see
And won't participate
I'm bubbling with emotions

When I don't smile, don't laugh, don't dance, won't talk
And can't love
I'm bubbling with emotions

When I can't think, can't dream, can't create,
can't be me and won't be bothered
I'm bubbling with emotions

When all I need is to find myself, to rediscover my being
To cherish the life, to discover my roots and
ain't allowed to be myself
I'm bubbling with emotions

About Friends

you were not a choice of the eyes,
but only what the soul could see,
you were not the person I would have chose,
for you were neither rich nor famous.
you were not the smartest person I know,
for although not dull,
you had not the sharpest brains around.

of the honorable man I know,
you couldn't stand head and shoulders with them,
what is it I saw,
that brought these two unlikely souls together?
maybe, it was you who befriended me or
it could have been the other way round.
with all your good judgement in character,
you could have done better but me.

a good sense of humor like yours could have
secured you a more lucrative prey.
my jaundiced judgement should have had you
buried with embarrassment.
my vile temperament should have sent you
looking for sanctuary.
against all odds, we were bonded together by choice,
for two people so different, it's an irony
to call us kindred spirits.

in times of sorrows and happiness, none is closer.
I wouldn't wish you to be big headed,
should I admit that life wouldn't be the same
without you.
I can however safely say, if I had to do it again,
I would choose you as a friend,
though I know not why.

I Can

Determination, the vehicle that gives wheels to dreams
Belief, the conviction that gives ideas the will to fly
Destiny, purpose beyond dreams of reality in my life time
Fulfillment, convictions of life worthier than a potential
Listen to me, for I know when I say,
I can

27-04

A long overdue birth, a pregnancy denied for far too long.
Midwives in denial, the haggling and
shifting for a final date.
Someone suggested that the baby was
not mature enough for delivery.
Another suggested the 27-04 as the date of delivery,
Others raised their hands in disbelief
at such a stupid suggestion.
Spectators predicted a catastrophic birth.
Some said, it was bound to be natural,
Others said, it would have to be by caesarian.
Others said, it matters not, 'cause both
mother and child won't make it.

It appeared as if none was ready for the too soon date,
Some midwives screaming, that otherwise
they are going to miss the delivery.
Others saying, the birth date was cast in stone,
the baby could not stay another day.
The labor pains long and painful.
Eventually! the day arrived, delivery proceeded as
unexpected, natural and to a healthy baby.
With the midwives assisting and co-operating
in ways nobody could have dreamt.
Spectators screamed miracle!
Was it or simply nature taking its cause?
Of a birth long overdue.
27-04-1994, the birth of a nation.

Honourable Intentions

I swear it was for the benefit of all
It was an act clothed with the best of intentions
Nobody was supposed to get injured
Friendships were not to be broken
Lovers were not to become enemies
Families were not to be estranged
Errors, misjudgments, deceits, and lies.

Strangers In Company

Fate; conspired us to meet.
We talked about:
Ideas and places, experiences and feelings,
Dreams and fears.
We learned about each other's:
Wishes and beliefs, origins and travels,
Abilities and knowledge.
We discovered each other's humanity,
In the distinctions that makes us similar,
The complexities that makes us individuals
And the lives that makes us mortals.
Providence had the upper hand.
Nothing could be more strange.

How Do We Extricate Ourselves?

"There is a fact: white men consider
themselves superior to black men.
There is another fact: black men want to prove to white
men, at all costs, the richness of their thoughts,
the equal value of their intellect.
How do we extricate ourselves?"
- Franz fanon

Where do we start, to remember who we
were, before we were exposed?
How do we begin to rediscover what it is that
we stood for, before we were educated?
What do we do to relearn what we stood for,
before we were taught what we lacked?
Who are we going to be, after we have
de-cultured to aspirations of civility?
When are we starting to live, by being as good as
we can be, without trying to better them?
How do we extricate ourselves?

This Feeling

I know not what it is, I feel for certain it won't go away
It instills fear in me, without the threat of harm
It has created a thirst in my soul, which
I cannot seem to quench
It has created a vacuum in my resolve,
that took away my self-sufficiency
It has violated my thoughts and left me a brooding hermit
It has left a gaping hole in my heart
and a lump in my throat
This feeling unknown to me, foreign and yet so familiar
This bittersweet feeling I'd rather not loose
It's a feeling cured only with your presence by my side
It's this feeling, those who know, call it love
It's a feeling, I will share only with you

Rumours Of War

IN THE LAND OF UR, Mesopotamia and Babylon,
There is an air of defiance, from New York to Paris
and London there is a move of desperation.
From Havana to Johannesburg and Berlin, the attitude is;
not in our names.
From Cape Town to Oslo, San Francisco to Beijing,
The message is; not in our names.

Rumors of war, warmongers and warlords gather
around like rain clouds before a storm.
In Riad and Kuwait City, the hawks gather in the
name of peace, we shall bomb Baghdad to freedom.
In the name of oil, we shall liberate you from yourselves
In fear's name, we demand you to be submissive.

Rumors of war, not in our names, say the doves,
The French, The Russians, The Chinese,
The Europeans and The Africans.
Not in our names, say the UN and the American people.
There are rumors of war in the land of Abraham.

History

It's his story; neither yours nor mine.
It's the story of the victors over the vanquished.
It's the story of the conquerors over the conquered.
It's the story of the slave traders over their human cargo.
It's the story of the slave masters about their slaves.
Masters of their own stories.

It's the story of the colonizers over the colonized.
It's the story of the civilized over the savages.
It's the story of the missionaries over the heathens.
It's the story of the discoverers over the discovered.
It's the story of the quagga and the dodo told by humans.
Masters of their own stories.

It's the story of the poor man told by the rich man.
It's the story of those with no past told by the present.
It's the story of you and me told by them.
It's their stories, neither yours nor mine.
Masters of their own stories.
Like an icon out of the ashes, we shall rise to tell
our stories.
The vanquished and the conquered, the human
cargo and the slaves, the colonized and the
discovered, the heathens and the savages, shall all
rise above being footnotes in their own stories.
We shall tell our own stories.

The Quagga and the Dodo, shall tell how
they roamed the plains of Africa.
The Khoi and the Aborigine, shall tell of
their days in harmony with nature.
Kunta Kinte and Nonqawuse, shall
tell us how it really happened.
Timbuktu and Mapungubwe, shall tell of their days of glory.
We shall tell our own stories.
A story of you and me.

Looking For Enlightment

Learning to see the light with the eye of the soul.
Discovering the self with the curiosity of a child.
Settling at a place where:
Pure thoughts flow like spring water in summer,
Dreams and wishes are bound together in reality,
Fear is unknown and contentment resides,
Belief alters the boundaries of the impossible,
Ideas reach maturity and happiness is not a distant
memory and love is bigger than the heart.
A place, where life is, more than just a gift horse.

Family

Branches of a single vine
Off-springs from a single line

Bonds without a weak link
Responsibilities assumed without a wink

Care received without being earned
Duty assumed without being learned

Diversity not turning into division
Misunderstandings straightened by communication

Sharing of experiences unforgettable
Distances that makes togetherness memorable

Pains that did not turn malignant
Disagreements that did not run rampant

Friendships cemented at birth
Love shared within the blood girth.

Talk To Me

Communicate with me when I appear list interested.
Don't talk to me like a negotiator.
Say to me how disgusted you are by my behavior.
Don't bargain with me like a salesman.
Shelter me not from the gossips you heard down the street.
Chastise me for being so disrespectful.
Congratulate me for having done so well.
Talk to me like a friend.

Don't be so condescending like an arbitrator.
Converse with me about your deepest darkest secrets.
Don't be intimidated by the material
wealth I have accumulated.
Tell me how disappointed you are, like you used to.
Speak to me when I appear to be the know all.
Persuade me when I m being big headed.
Show me the way when I go astray.
Talk to me like a brother.

Don't be so neutral like a mediator.
Convince me of the morality of our people.
Don't be bothered by the gray hair on my head.
Encourage me when I'm on the right.
Whisper to me in the ear when I embarrass you.
Laugh with me on those joyous moments.
Cry with me when the clouds are dark.
Talk to me like you are my son.

Be patient with me when I'm being disagreeable.
Teach me the ways of our people.
Don't give up on me when you are
convinced I can't be helped.
Pray with me when my spirit needs healing.
Stand by me when my knees look shaky.
Celebrate with me for goals attained.
Share with me the warmth in your heart.
Talk to me like you are my parent.

Cheer with me in celebration.
Don't be overwhelmed by my recent achievements.
Sing for me when I can't sleep.
Smile at me when I make you happy.
Hold my hand when I need you by my side.
Make me know how you really feel.
Believe in me when I need encouragement.
Talk to me like you are my lover.

Time Will Tell

Nobody will be there to say I told you so.
Sad we didn't learn from our past.
Is it the relativity of time that breeds complacency,
or the conspiracy of the familiar that makes
growth looks retarded under a watchful eye?
Forget not what they taught you, every Goliath
has a David; remember every dog has its day.

Stand-up and speak-up or forever:
Be locked in the gallows of regrets for donating the
legacy of future generations to political hooligans,
Be enslaved in a mental Babylon for squandering
our Fathers hard-earned freedom,
Be dangled by the hangman's noose for allowing
the do-gooders to desecrate our brothers'
rights in the name of keeping peace.
Suffer perpetual prejudice for being born
in the belly side of the earth.

"Oh! Time alone, oh! Time will tell."

The Trip

Something about motion sickness, a little about
seclusion, a lot about being idle in a state of
Motion, brings the best and worst in people.
Strangers sharing padkos, ideas being exchanged
without prejudice, people coming out of
Their cocoons, loves and hates being declared
In their nakedness.
Something about being away from home, makes
people wants to forget their miseries, encourages
people to confide in each other and allows people to
be themselves without the fear of being judged.
Something about the journey makes
the destination irrelevant.
Something about the trees and mountains passing
through your window makes you want
To go on forever.

Take A Look Inside

Some things are better not said, for the
rift that may result may be a gulf.
Some feelings are better not shown, for the
embarrassment may be too shameful.
Some dreams are best forgotten for their revealing
May be a cancer.
What I saw in your eyes scared me so.
What I felt in my heart left me a different person.
What I heard from your voice left me a non-believer.
The stalemate in our situation petrified me.
The conspiracy against our instincts is murderous.
The cover-up against our feelings is immoral.
Too much time spent on being cautious,
Too much energy wasted on keeping face,
Too much effort squandered on being prim and proper.
Our expectations of the real borders on sinful,
Our take on this life smacks of outrageous greed,
Our beliefs in ourselves aren't worth a penny at the market.
How sad, for all the love we had.

The Players

Soldiers without countries, in a war without enemies.
Fighting for a cause best not defined.
These are villains of the heart, poachers of morality
and looters of order and family values.
Their wishes are their pickings, a heart is best bought
with a purse, words betray the conscience.
Men and women without feelings, for it's a
gamblers rule, never to play with your emotions,
for should the game be lost, so is your soul.

In hush-hush tones, whisper the commoners,
Here come the players, brinkmanship is their game.
Casanova and Gigolo would have
hanged their heads in shame.
This breed will put their heads and lives in the guillotine
for a piece of fun, 'cause they know what the game is worth,
Nothing is worth the soul.

If! Of Love

If I had known how to say it, I would have told
you the first time I laid my eyes on you.
If I had had the dictionary of emotions, I
would have told you how I felt then.
If I had had the courage, I would have defied my body
when it decided to get paralyzed with emotions.

My life took a new turn, when our eyes met.
My heart opened up new doors when you smiled at me.
My soul jumped up in celebration, for
having shared the earth with you.

I know it is within you to forgive me, for being just human.
I know you saw it in my eyes that the person within
me was screaming at the top of my emotions.
I know your heart responded with joy
for the tears in your eyes said so.

Verily I say to you today, what this body was trying to say,
was to get out these three little words: "I LOVE YOU".

At The Back Of The Mind

Should you ask me, I would say it sounds suspicious.
Should you tell anybody, they will say,
it was probably a bad dream.
Should you think about it, you will
believe you are going crazy.
The present stands uncertain and the future
looms confused as if it wasn't meant to be.
At the back of the mind, there lies at the bottom
of it all, something bigger than you and me.
Fate; destiny written in the stars.
Coincidence; encounters bigger than chance.
Opportunity; the future in the land of the open minded.
At the back of the mind, the truth lies
dormant like a sleeping volcano.

For Fear Of The Truth

News best not known
A past best buried
It's a life you rather not have had
They say ignorance is bliss
A future crammed with uncertainties
It's the adventure to the unknown land
You don't need to go there
They say what you do not know cannot hurt you
For the truth is a matter of perception

For Us All

Things you ain't supposed to see,
Voices you ain't supposed to hear
Words you ain't supposed to say
You are just human
The life, the love, the beliefs
Which are truly not yours
The truth you need not know
You don't need to know

Lessons From Beyond

Sometimes I sit and wonder, about the purpose of it all
Of the normal doings, the normal behavior and
The normal happenings
I marvel at the logic of it all
The unquestioned acceptance of what is
The undoubted following of the norm
The revered worship of the moral code
I'm humbled by those who have the dogma over our
behaviors, our thoughts, our feelings, our ideas
And even our dreams
I'm stunned by our submissiveness at the feet of
those who hold the gospel truth, at our conformity
without question, our reasoning lost without
wonder, our beliefs disappeared without a trace.
But then, who am I.

Be Not Afraid

Of your thoughts running astray,
Of your ideas escaping captivity,
Of your dreams going beyond the permissible,
Be not afraid
When you discover what you were not meant to see,
When you stumble across forbidden truth,
When you slide into uncontrollable feelings,
Be not afraid
Of the image in the mirror
Of the shadow on the ground
Of the reflection in the pool
Be not afraid
For what you see is the real you.

The Discovery

The other day I made a startling discovery.
I saw life for what it is.
An instinctive drive in the path of righteousness,
A compass of the conscience pointed to
the true north of our beings,
Feelers of the heart in the paved roads of the soul,
Eyes seeing without shadows, ears hearing without echoes.
I discovered of:
A truth covered in different shades,
Love carried in a basket of conditions,
Belief enslaved into perpetual bondage by fear,
A morality ghost from a long abandoned society,
My unclothed self in the garden of good.
I lost my blissful ignorance and hid away from my Creator.
I learned from you, of my damning nakedness.

Tomorrow

That land of the optimist, that place in time we need
to arrive prepared, that future you need to know
now. Maybe I need to go see a prophet, a seer will
do, A gypsy can read some cards or a palm reader,
Let an astrologer read the stars for me or maybe
some bones by an inyanga can tell a better story.

That desire as old as mankind, who will be there?
Who are the new kings and queens and most importantly
What shall my share be, in that land of tomorrow?
Where my miseries would have disappeared, my hunger
vanished, my past forgotten and I the person in charge.
I need to know of that day after tomorrow,
I need to be prepared and ready.
I need to know of that day when I will have my
place in the sun, in that day over the horizon.

That is, and only if the day won't be dark and gloomy,
If the pasture will be green and bountiful,
If I will be living in the land of milk and honey and
my streets paved with gold, if I could evade the dark
clouds coming towards me, if I could cheat death.
That is, in that land of tomorrow, if only I could know,
I will live for then and now wouldn't hurt so much.

Often Is Not Enough

When practice fails to make perfect
Experience is not gained by exposure
Mistakes are not lessons learned
Déjà vu is worse than repetition
Trial and error is but an endless nightmare
And life is everything but a dream
Then we know; often is not enough.

Politicos

Firstly, they shifted the goal posts.
Then they changed the language to suit their needs.
The rest of us ended up speaking in tongues and
Now we can't hear ourselves think, our
hearts talking to us, our children cry, our
communication scrambled in modernity.

They called it equality, until they ran out of things to equal.
Then they called it feminism, until typhoons became male.
Morals and manners undressed in public and
religion deconstructed, everything caged into
Right and wrong, mostly wrong.

Then simplicity was replaced by complicasy,
Ordinary words swallowed by dictionarial
Monstrosities, meaning intimidated by repercussions,
Now we don't mean what we say,
And we don't say what we mean nor do we
Intend as we thought or act as we intend.
We now speak politicos.
This is the twelfth official language.

The dictionary is as amended, human
beings have become hu-person
short, is vertically disadvantaged,
Theft, is affirmative distribution,
Stupidity, is intellectually un-empowered and
Comrade citizen, has metamorphosed
into fellow parliamentarian.

Words are given a free reign, the interpreter
leads the speaker, the singer follows the
dancer, we now speak from the mouth,
Let the head and heart follow from behind.

Talking has become a dangerous business,
Language an engaging exercise, aesthetically perfect,
Societal aligned, democratically balanced
And politically correct.
We have turned foreigners within ourselves.
We now live in the era of politicos,
A language made to order.

The Judas Song

An opportunity lost to political enthusiasts.
Now bound into a promise we didn't make,
Conned into a history we fought against,
Sold for a song to the gods of reconciliation,
We have become a nation without a soul.

Sounding like two rivers heading in opposite directions,
Oil and water tied together by fear,
Our disbelief bludgeoned into submission
by the patriotic hammer,
Our fists unbundled into begging
hands with promises of glory,
Our African rhythm devoured by foreign drums.

Fed to us like poison medicine,
Grudgingly we swallowed to remain patriotic zombies,
Blood and sweat of hector Peterson,
Steve Biko and Chris Hani washed
of our collective memories.
The song they swore by gambled on
the bargaining table at Codesa.

Old Sontoga must be turning in his grave.
"Nkosi sikeleli Africa"; our song of freedom betrayed.

I Slumbered On

In the early hours of a May Day,
There I was on a pilgrimage in Bethlehem.
I looked around at my compatriots, their
singing subdued by the earliness of the hour,
the cold and the darkness helping along,
We huddled together like sheep in the rain,
The chitchat of those not in slumber drowned
by the road and engine noises.
If only we had known, I slumbered along.
In a mixture of dreams and thoughts:
I saw my beloved and daughter back in Kimberly in
a cocoon of peace that touched my inner being. My
extended hand only brought me to my present reality,
The seat in front and the mist outside.
My feelings of time and place suspended in
an unending journey in the clouds.
I overhear a conversation between comrades on the other
seat, it is going to be an unforgettable experience and
another comrade responding, "indeed, a day to remember."
Their conversation brought a shiver through my
body, which I could only interpret as excitement.
Little did we know. I slumbered on.
Jolted into wakefulness by the roughness of the
road below, a voice from the back yelling,
"driver, waar gaan ons nou", somebody from the
front next to the driver responding, "sorry comrades
we missed a turn in the mist, these road signs are not
visible, the driver is just trying to make a turn and we

shall be back in the main road in no time." by now
our slumbers had disappeared and a chorus of
protestations mounting.
screams! screams! splash!
Confusion, comrades everywhere, running backward
and forward, others climbing over seats and windows.
I set paralyzed in my seat, the engine ceased,
I felt wetness in my feet that made my heart sink.
Water coming in through each and every opening.
I thought of my dear beloved and my
little girl, they looked even further.
The only words I could think of, 'don't
worry we shall overcome'.
In that same seat, in that unfortunate bus, in
the soon to be infamous, Saulspoor dam, a
memorable May Day.
I slumbered on…

A Gift Unusual

It was a surprise of surprises.
The covering could have fooled one, there was none at all.
The size astounded me, it was neither big nor small.
The beauty eternal, beyond description.
The feeling, life changing,
It touched my soul.
How do I thank thee?
For such a magnanimous offering

The need is acknowledged, I can't
imagine how it was before.
I'm honored for the care you entrusted in me.
I'm humbled to have shared on such a precious gift.
I will cherish this present for all the days to come.
I'm blessed for the love of this gift extraordinaire.

Take Me Not For Granted

Forget me not 'cause I'm always on your side
Acquire not a blind sport for me for being there for too long
Judge not my ideas, by the number of books passed
Dismiss me not, for my lack of
proficiency in a foreign language
Presume not my experiences, by the moons I have lived
Hear me out, even though I lack the expertise you demand
Give me a hearing, regardless of the value of my possessions
Learn my character, not from what you
heard but from what you saw
Judge my ideas by their content not origin
Determine my intelligence independently of the test
Live above the stereotypes and open your eyes
Take me not for granted
Maybe, just maybe, you can learn a thing or two

Thank You

'Be thankful for what is given, however
do not be overly thankful
For you may undermine the generosity of the giver'
Kalil Gibran -the prophet

How do I thank thee? How do I thank thee;
For being there when most needed
For saying the right words when least expected
For listening when no one would
For caring without expecting anything in return?
How do I thank thee? How do I thank thee;
For the kindness of your words
For the compassion in your voice
For the gentleness in you touch
For the love in your eyes?

How do I thank thee; without offending
the generosity of your heart?
Thank you

Weapons Of Mass Destruction

These are those we look for
The once we say what they are
The once we say you have
The once you shouldn't deny you posses
The once you shouldn't have

Defined as anything that flies
Anything that looks threatening
Anything that could kill
Anything you cannot justify
Anything we told you, you shouldn't have
Everything we suspect you have

We shall search for it
Look for it, hunt for it and interrogate for it
If we don't find it
We shall bomb you with our smart bombs
E-bombs and radio active bombs
We shall send you back to the Stone Age
For only we can posses weapons of mass destruction.

Truth That Hurts

A lie born of good intentions
A bad habit to maintain good relations
A flutter to cheer a sad neighbor
Condolences to an undeserving bereaved

Friendships built on false pretences
Relationships failing on mutual respect
A dependency that reeks of addiction
A mole in the palace of trust

A family consumed with blind reverence
Old skeletons bundled in family cupboards
Young truth buried with whispers in the dark
Quarrels unresolved turned into tumors by procrastination

A sour romance disguised in the mask of happy love
An old boat sailing on memory alone
An alliance of the hearts betrayed by mediocrity
Suffocation in the bag of normality
Truth bludgeoned on the altar of expediency
It's mendacity on a grand scale

Prejudice

A state of mind perpetuated by a fear of the self
A belief dished in plates of ignorance
A virus feeding on our inability to tolerate differences
An individual's illness mirroring a societal ghost
A what-if, magnified beyond a conviction
Hate, masquerading as fair play
Desperation, propped-up as live debate
Frustrations raised under the banner of rights
Greed, feasting at the table of need
Racism, whitewashed in pictures of nationalism
It's pride of the self converted to the
non-existence of the other.

We Crossed

If our paths crossed in the tapestry of humanity,
Our souls were intertwined in the rug of spirituality.
We shall forever remain a work of art
in the market of universality.

In This Together

In the blink of an eye, we fall in
Hook, line, sinker & angler
It's a life time experience
It's you and me re-writing the rules
Tell me about it

Hope

A seed borne of optimism
A dream of a future filled with happiness
A sanctuary to hide away from an unpleasant reality
A guiding rope leading to the end of the tunnel
An expression of belief in the existence of good
An attribute of humanity that redefines the species
The cause and content of the reason to survive
The bread and butter of revolutionaries
The heart and soul of humanitarians
The nucleus of our spiritual universe

A Tribute To An African Girl Child

IF I WHERE YOU…
I would look at this world with bright open eyes
I would walk out of inferiority and degradation
I would conquer poverty and its accomplices
I would carry my head high and be
proud to be an African daughter.

I would defy the odds like it's been done before
I would try my luck and stand on an anthill to be counted
I would learn the ways of the world from friends
And foes alike
I would stand head and shoulders with the rest of them
Just like an African daughter.

I would live a footprint enough to
nourish the next generation
I would live a legacy sufficient for a clan
I would redefine the rules for an African
child to stand on equal footing
I would treat my brothers and sisters
with respect, love and dignity
The way only an African daughter can.

The Price Of The Bride

Love, committed in the number of herds
A family bond, inseparable by divorce
A commitment, more valuable than the price of rubies
An exchange of values, worthier than a batter
It's lobola, an African tradition

Reduced to a commodity, costlier than gold
Subdued to a market, busier than the
Johannesburg stock exchange
Impoverished to a game of chance,
better than the July handicap
Degraded into a once of chance, most
probable than the lotto
It's lobola, an African tradition
It's marriage in the - century

I Am Grateful

I was attacked, stabbed and dispossessed of my belongings.
You said I should be thankful 'cause it was
just a phone and some change.
Everybody agreed how lucky I was 'cause the
stab wound in my hand wasn't fatal.
I the victim, I'm grateful.

I was raped, beaten-up and left for dead.
The nurses and doctors called me a fighter.
The counselors and psychologists called me a survivor.
Friends and family were humbled by my bravery.
I the victim, I'm grateful.

I was Hi-jacked, shot-at and left on the roadside.
The police said how fortunate I was because
another couple died there last week.
The insurance said I should be thankful
to Net-star for recovering my car.
I the victim, I'm grateful.

I am grateful for being robbed, stabbed,
raped, hijacked and shot at.
I am grateful to be the lucky victim,
the one you didn't bury.

On Whose Side Are You?

I always thought you were on my side
Until I saw you laugh with the other side
That was before I heard you sell them to their enemies
Then you convinced me of your true side
Only to stab me in the back
All I beg of you is to know
On whose side are you?

Lady Justice

My humble upbringing failed to prepare me for this.
Of my chance encounter with lady justice.

The purposefulness of the men and women
in black gowns seemed otherworldly.
The seriousness of the men in uniform
melted away my confidence.
The shackled arms and feet of my brothers
and sisters left me confused.
The raised call for silence sent a shiver through my body.

The humble appearance of the man in the red
robes failed to ease my apprehension.
The call for my name to go take the stand
could have come from God himself.
My two hands could both have been left
when I was asked to raise the right one.
My voice abandoned me when I needed it most.

The look on the face of the man in chains said it all.
I cursed my eyes for seeing too much.
I should have closed my eyes when I saw this man
Shoot my father.
Now here is my punishment for talking too much.
I should tell of my father's death to the world.
I am the child witness.

About Time

"The other day they came to fetch my neighbor, they
said he was a communist. I kept quite because I wasn't.
Then they came for me…" Unknown

It's about time, you and me stop waiting our turn.
Time to start telling what's bugging us.
Time to confess our beliefs without being ashamed.
Time to have an opinion that carries our convictions.
Time to raise our long overdue objections.

It's about time, I start speaking on my neighbor's behalf.
Time I stop watching my brother being
exploited in the name of employment.
Time I raise my hand against perpetual
bondage named capitalist realities.
Time we stop the tide against the engulfing globalization.
It's about time, I start being my brother's keeper.

A Borrowed Life

When you look across your neighborhood
and you don't belong.
When your neighbor's dogs bark at you
because you look unfamiliar.
When your house is twice the size of its inhabitants.
When you feel desperate in your attempts to be you.
When your children wish you were poor so
they would have a normal neighborhood.
When you are ashamed to spend time with your childhood
friends because you believe they would ask you for money.
When your success feels unreal because
you are one in a million.
Then you should know, yours is a borrowed life my friend.

The Quest

In an endless horizon the pursuit of the
running breeze seems much easier.
I followed with the conviction of a Jesuit priest;
Only if I had understood the purpose of the chase.
The ancients knew the meaning of a mirage and understood
that the only thirst it ever quenches is that of longing.
I persisted filled with hope of an oasis
over the dunes where none existed.

A pot of gold at the end of the rainbow was the promise.
Where I come from rainbows had no end.
My desire for fulfillment flee out of
my hands like a butterfly.
Only if I had known that the victory
in this struggle lies within.
Only if I had known that the mountain
to be conquered is within.
Only if I had known I could have fought
this enemy with more understanding.

Anger Management

Don't calm me down when I rapture into volcanic rage.
Don't put out my fire when I flare up like straw hut.
Don't put me on Prozac when I sink to
the bottom like a river diamond.
Don't smoother my laughter when I scream
like a baboon on a Marula tree.

Let me have my highs and lows with maximum emotion.
Let my eyes shed their tears till I'm drowned.
Let my voice be heard over the
mountains like an African drum.
Let my brooding be mine without
being diagnosed as a sickness.

Let me conquer my own demons
and wake the child within.

Not Above Extinction

Homo Sapiens cries! Above extinction!
Maybe, but not its behaviors, those attributes that
defined the species disappearing like dinosaurs of old

Humanity, gone out of fashion decades ago
Respect, a burden never understood
by the young of the species
Care, a word abandoned like the elders and the frail
Courtesy, the left over from road rage
Love, what Romeo and Juliet took to their graves
Dignity, a hat one once wore to show humility earned
Understanding, the only hill that stood taller than pride

Not extinct we cry
Self-inhalation it seems, but this species seems
irrevocably redefined and its behavior
is not above extinction

Remember To Forget

You said that you were forgiving me
I thanked you for doing so
We agreed we were going to bury the hatchet
The world looked at us for reconciliation and forgiveness

You don't let me forget how unjust I was to you
You don't stop to make me feel
uncomfortable about my property
You keep embarrassing me when I
am being courteous to you
When are you going to forget the past and move-on?

I shall remember to remind you until
you stop patronizing me
I shall remind you until you begin to understand my pain
I shall poke fun at your looks of concern
until I sleep with a full stomach
I shall remember to remind you, until you learn
to feel what I meant when I said I forgive you.

The Modern Day Slave

My ancestors were enslaved in body
and mind against their will,
They were hunted, captured and sold as beasts of burden.
Against their will, they were taught a new
language of the whip and the gun.
Against all odds their spirits and souls
refused to be conquered and subdued.

I am the modern day slave and proud of it.
My education was my capture, sold for
employment and credit is my master.
Voluntarily, I submit myself deep into debt for a mansion
over my head and garments of silk over my body.
Everyday I borrow my way around for the most
sumptuous meals and the finest Scotch.
To the highest bidder, I offer what is
left of my tormented soul.

I'm the modern day slave, turned into
a house-slave of co-operation.
I'm a willing slave, chained into luxury
by gold and platinum cards.
My bondage has no freedom in sight.

Racist Hunt

Have you heard?
A bearded racist discovered in the Springboks.
A racist has been declared says SARFU.
A racist has been confirmed says Media.
Thrown out, fired, castrated and gone for good.
Hurrah! to SARFU, applaud the politicians.

Woo! Not so quick.
No racist found retracts SARFU.
Smoke without fire, man cleared and apologies in order.
Matter is closed and no resignations expected.
Maybe a formal witch hunt, oops! We
mean a racist hunt will do.

An elusive animal this racist.
Where art though racist?
Has anybody seen a racist?

That; Leaves Me Cold

A chilling African spring night.
A naked battered body, lying on the back of a bakkie.
A cracked skull to reveal all the black consciousness ideas.
Misery and death hardly a trophy.
"Death by misadventure", says the coroner.
"That; leaves me cold", says the Minister.

Embedded

Prophets of truth or distributors of ruse
On the side of truth or the left side of right
At the forefront and the trenches or
The underside of the propaganda machine
Hunting for the truth with Al-Jazeera or
Feeding of the Coalition Truth
Embedded or in bed with Bush and Blair

This Day

Is this a day of remembrance or a day of reckoning?
The day humanity was attacked or
the day the truth resurfaced?
A day the world was held hostage or
the day the myth was deflated?

Were new enemies made or did old skeletons fell out?
Was history implicated or just the future being muddied?
Terror to all peace loving people or a
coming home to roost time?

Is this Day a day of Chilean irresponsibility
Afghani subjugation or American hypocrisy?
Is this day a day like any other?

Soul Revolution

A migration of beliefs contrary to nature

At a time of spiritual maturity
Hate and suspicion have formed an impeccable alliance
When the world has enough food
Greed and gluttony have conspired to starve the rest
In a world where plague is curable
Healers and merchants are holding the sick to ransom
Where diamonds are forever
They are polished with the blood of the
poor on whose land they grew
When a nation's oil riches
Is a curse inviting enemies and warmongers

A soul revolution is underway
Heed thy soul and follow thy heart
Tomorrow is the day you have been promised
This Prophesy shall be fulfilled…

Them That Matters

All those important people I know

Them politicians that I brush shoulders with
Them celebrities that remembers my name
Them rich folks that calls me asking for favors
Them fellows on TV that I can 'Truly'
claim we grew-up together
Them beauty queens I rather be seen with
Them famous people at whose parties I'm seen
Them intellectuals on whose name dropping I'm sustained
Even them notorious 'cause they have power

Only THEM that matters I'll claim as my friends

Johnny Has Arrived

Johnny come lately
Johnny is here
Johnny missed the gravy train
Johnny caught the BEE train

Johnny a communist no more
Johnny is a free marketer today
Johnny the shop steward is history
Johnny is company executive with a conscience

Johnny the penniless of student days
Johnny is a dollar millionaire
Johnny the community leader in the township
Johnny is the mayor of a small town

Watch your left, watch your right
And don't forget your back
Johnny is coming right at you
Johnny has arrived

Fear

A vicious animal indeed
Indiscriminate in its attacks
Paralyzing in effect
A parasite on one's conscience
Devours the mind from within
Turns brave men into squeamish kids
Spreads around like a bad rumor
More contagious than Sars
Gobbles dreams like a shark
Invisible like the man-eaters of Tsavo
Attacks by stealth to the unsuspecting
Buries its victims with the rage of a volcano
Yet its motive remains unknown
And yes, curable, with just a grain of belief.

Tread Carefully

(in memory of Lizani)

We lived with caution, he lived with abandon.
We lived for days to come,
He lived as if there was no tomorrow.
We held back, he was extravagant.
We feared the unknown, he thrived in it.
We understood impossibilities,
He lived in the world of the possible.
We taught him of human boundaries,
He showed us the borderless of the achievable.
We treaded carefully; he boldly left his footprints.
We made him feel special; he glorified us for knowing him.

Then Came Us

When hope, was a long lost memory
Understanding, a foreign concept
Negotiation, a finger pointing anomaly
Trust, a fools dream

Then came us:
We talked when we shouldn't
We listened when we should be arguing
We negotiated when we should be fighting
We trusted when it was ill advised
We dare hoped when what we needed was a miracle

Then came us:
Bucking the trend
Talking about forgiveness
Believing in truth and reconciliation
Suggesting of things called Ubuntu
Feeling smug about our beliefs
But then we are South Africans and
We have ten years to show for it

The Other Side

The other side of our mental image
The dark side to our positive emotions
Pools of anger we should never visit
Pits of fear we should never fall into
Waves of hate in proportions unparalleled

A push we should deny till eternity
To the other side of the humanity mirror
Resist we should at all costs
From slipping down the slippery slope to the abyss
Poisoned beliefs, a raging fire unchecked
Desperation magnified to mountainous proportions

The other side we should not visit
The other side to the human soul
The other side to persons we were born to be
May we never get there.

If Truth Be Told

WE WISH…

If only we knew the truth
Our difficulties wouldn't be too hard to bear
Our lives would be plain and straight forward
We would tell foe and friend as black from white
Our beliefs would set us free

If truth be told…
Heartbreaks and betrayals would be laid bear
Pasts and secrets would be confessed
Longings and desires would be displayed in the open
We may have to forgo our little white lies

Beautiful And Delicious Thorns

A bed well made but not to be lied on
It's a bed of roses pleasing to the eye,
Sweet to the nose, thorny to lie on.

A fruit with a name of dubious origin,
A pear only in shape,
Demanding masterly skills for approach
Reduces eating to an achievement,
Prickly pear;
Not a fruit to gobble.

No

May I learn to:
Say no, without a coma
Say no, without prejudice
Say no, to mean what I intend

May I not be intimidated away from it
May I say no, without guilt
May I say no, with honesty
May I not mince my words in saying no
May no, be the yes, to the desires of my soul.
May I say no, without deceiving myself
May I learn to say, NO, NO, and NO
Without shame

May We Be:

The purpose beyond the means
The reach over the hand
The achievement above the goal
The life of the worth
The dreams of the desired
The feelings of the denied
The ideals of the enlightened

Can we be:-

The architects of memory
The draughtsman of ideas
The blueprint of beliefs
The strategy to a battle
The destination reached
The deliverance to a wish
All we need be, without loosing the self.

A Place We Called Our Own

Politicians and journalists, lawyers and civil servants,
Rich and poor, honest citizen and the riff-raffs,
All brushed shoulders at Off-Moroka.

Musicians and poets, photographers and painters,
Film makers and story tellers,
All displayed their wares at Off-Moroka.

Mnushu and Mielie-Bread, food for the masses,
Spicy chips and tingling curry, tantalized the taste buds,
Expensive beer and cheap wine, drowned
the patrons at Off-Moroka.

Regis House on Adderley Street, Cape Town,
Hold good memories,
A place we called our own.

The Gloom

On top are the clueless
Propping them are the fraudsters
Cheering them are the gullible
The brave shovel the stink upwards
Dante's hell would melt into submission
The ignoramus are choked in blissful happiness
To the distant observer, it's a dung heap
It's the curse of democracy
Let each fool exercise his right to be foolish.

The Warmth In Your Eyes

I may have said something enticing, I may have
said something rhythmic or I may have said
something romantic, But that was not it.
It may have been your comment, It may have been your
nudge or It may have been my courage, But I doubt it
I suspect it was the warmth in your eyes
that reminded me who I was,
the warmth in your eyes that reaffirmed
that you are here to stay or
The warmth in your eyes that said I'm yours forever.

Once In A Lifetime

They said, once in a lifetime, there
will be an event to remember.
No one imagined it will be one felt by the entire world;
until an invisible enemy called SARS Covid-19 arrived.
A Greek tragedy of mythical proportions, nicknamed
Alpha, Kappa, Delta and Omicron. People drowning
and suffocating in open air, coughing and sneezing
to their families and neighbours' demise.
Causing death and destruction in its path,
laying waste to countries rich and poor. Bringing down
economies and empires to their knees. Villages, towns and
cities indefinitely closed for business. Churches, Mosques
and Temples unceremoniously closed for worship.
Cars, buses, boats, trains and planes, grounded.
Doors, gates and borders, bolted and locked.
With soap and water, mask and sanitizer,
oxygen and vaccine, humanity prevailed.
A once in a lifetime occurrence, a lesson of the century.